MARK

20 STUDIES FOR INDIVIDUALS AND GROUPS

N. T. WRIGHT

WITH LIN JOHNSON

IVP Connect

An imprint of InterVarsity Press
Downers Grove, Illinois

InterVarsity Press
P.O. Box 1400, Downers Grove, IL 60515-1426
World Wide Web: www.ivpress.com
E-mail: email@ivpress.com

InterVarsity Press® is the book-publishing division of InterVarsity Christian Fellowship/USA®, a movement of students and faculty active on campus at hundreds of universities, colleges and schools of nursing in the United States of America, and a member movement of the International Fellowship of Evangelical Students. For information about local and regional activities, write Public Relations Dept., InterVarsity Christian Fellowship/USA, 6400 Schroeder Rd., P.O. Box 7895, Madison, WI 53707-7895, or visit the IVCF website at <www.intervarsity.org>.

Cover design: Cindy Kiple
Cover image: MedioImages/Corbis
Interior image: Clipart.com

ISBN 978-0-8308-2182-2

Printed in the United States of America ∞

| P | 19 | 18 | 17 | 16 | 15 | 14 | 13 | 12 | 11 | 10 | 9 | 8 | 7 | 6 | 5 |
| Y | 26 | 25 | 24 | 23 | 22 | 21 | 20 | 19 | 18 | 17 | 16 | 15 | 14 | | |

CONTENTS

GETTING THE MOST OUT OF MARK

Mark's Gospel is the shortest and sharpest of the early stories about Jesus. Many people think Mark's Gospel was the first to be written, and certainly it has all the zip and punch of a quick story that's meant to grab you by the collar and make you face the truth about Jesus, about God and about yourself.

There is a sense of urgency in the Gospel of Mark. We find the word *immediately* many times in the first two chapters and several times after that. Early in chapter 1 the main theme of Jesus' ministry is articulated: God's kingdom is arriving. The kingdom of God is at hand (1:15). Something momentous is happening. Be alert! The train is about to leave the station. Jump on board before it is too late!

What was the crisis? For the century or so before Jesus' time the whole region had been overrun by the Romans. The legions had marched in and taken over, as they did everywhere from Britain to Egypt. Whoever got in their way was crushed. A few people—local politicians, tax collectors, call girls—did all right out of the Romans. Most people, though, saw them as The Enemy. As satan incarnate. They longed to see the Romans pushed out of the land. Rome was the Monster of all monsters. Rome was unclean. Rome was a nation of pigs. And like the pigs into which Jesus sent the legion of demons who were possessing the Gentile man in Mark 5, they should be thrown back into the Mediterranean Sea.

But here they were, the people of God, his chosen nation, and yet the land he'd given them, promised them, was occupied by enemies. Where was God? Why did he not act? Why were they in exile in their own land? The solution for many was to take up arms against Rome, violently expel it and restore God's kingdom.

Jesus knew, however, that this path on which Israel was heading with her Roman oppressors was a battle they would be sure to lose. Rome was simply too strong and too ruthless. Yes, God promised his kingdom, but it would not be the political, military kingdom they expected. And yes, the kingdom would come through the Messiah but not through the kind of Messiah they expected either. (For more on this letter, also see my *Mark for Everyone* on which this guide is based, published by SPCK and Westminster John Knox.)

For there was an enemy far more powerful than Rome that had to be dealt with—the satan. All of these forces were heading to an imminent climax. So this redefined kingdom must be announced immediately, before it was too late. Through this guide, prepared with the help of Lin Johnson for which I am grateful, we will see what this kingdom would look like and what the king would do in the story Mark tells us.

SUGGESTIONS FOR INDIVIDUAL STUDY

1. As you begin each study, pray that God will speak to you through his Word.

2. Read the introduction to the study and respond to the "Open" question that follows it. This is designed to help you get into the theme of the study.

3. Read and reread the Bible passage to be studied. Each study is designed to help you consider the meaning of the passage in its context. The commentary and questions in this guide are based on my own translation of each passage found in the companion volume to this guide in the For Everyone series on the New Testament (published by SPCK and Westminster John Knox).

4. Write your answers to the questions in the spaces provided or in a personal journal. Each study includes three types of questions: observation questions, which ask about the basic facts in the passage; interpretation questions, which delve into the meaning of the passage; and application questions, which help you discover the implications of the text for growing in Christ. Writing out your responses can bring clarity and deeper understanding of yourself and of God's Word.

5. Each session features selected comments from the For Everyone series. These notes provide further biblical and cultural background and contextual information. They are designed not to answer the questions for you but to help you along as you study the Bible for yourself. For even more reflections on each passage, you may wish to have on hand a copy of the companion volume from the For Everyone series as you work through this study guide.

6. Use the guidelines in the "Pray" section to focus on God, thanking him for what you have learned and praying about the applications that have come to mind.

SUGGESTIONS FOR GROUP MEMBERS

1. Come to the study prepared. Follow the suggestions for individual study mentioned above. You will find that careful preparation will greatly enrich your time spent in group discussion.

2. Be willing to participate in the discussion. The leader of your group will not be lecturing. Instead, she or he will be asking the questions found in this guide and encouraging the members of the group to discuss what they have learned.

3. Stick to the topic being discussed. These studies focus on a particular passage of Scripture. Only rarely should you refer to other portions of the Bible or outside sources. This allows for everyone to participate on equal ground and for in-depth study.

4. Be sensitive to the other members of the group. Listen attentively when they describe what they have learned. You may be surprised

by their insights! Each question assumes a variety of answers. Many questions do not have "right" answers, particularly questions that aim at meaning or application. Instead the questions push us to explore the passage more thoroughly.

When possible, link what you say to the comments of others. Also, be affirming whenever you can. This will encourage some of the more hesitant members of the group to participate.

5. Be careful not to dominate the discussion. We are sometimes so eager to express our thoughts that we leave too little opportunity for others to respond. By all means participate! But allow others to also.

6. Expect God to teach you through the passage being discussed and through the other members of the group. Pray that you will have an enjoyable and profitable time together, but also that as a result of the study you will find ways that you can take action individually and/ or as a group.

7. It will be helpful for groups to follow a few basic guidelines. These guidelines, which you may wish to adapt to your situation, should be read at the beginning of the first session.

   • Anything said in the group is considered confidential and will not be discussed outside the group unless specific permission is given to do so.

   • We will provide time for each person present to talk if he or she feels comfortable doing so.

   • We will talk about ourselves and our own situations, avoiding conversation about other people.

   • We will listen attentively to each other.

   • We will be very cautious about giving advice.

Additional suggestions for the group leader can be found at the back of the guide.

1

The Good News
of Jesus

Mark 1:1-45

You are sound asleep and dreaming, when suddenly the door bursts open and a bright light shines full in your face. A voice, breaking in on your dream-world, shouts, "Wake up! Get up! You'll be late!" And without more ado, the speaker splashes your face with cold water to make the point. Time to stop dreaming and face the most important day of your life.

That's what the opening of Mark's Gospel is like. Mark begins with John the Baptist's ministry, which was like throwing cold water on the surprised Jewish world. Many had been looking for a sign from God, but they hadn't expected it to look like this. Many had wanted a Messiah to lead them against the Romans, but they weren't anticipating a prophet telling them to repent.

OPEN

If someone woke you up and told you that the president or the prime minister or a prince was on his or her way to visit you, how would you respond?

STUDY

1. *Read Mark 1:1-13.* John the Baptist was Jesus' cousin on his mother's side, born a few months before Jesus. His ministry was to get people ready for the greatest moment in Jewish history, in world history: Jesus' ministry and then death and resurrection.

   How does John seek to prepare the people for Jesus' coming (vv. 1-8)?

2. The main thing Mark gets us to do in this opening passage is to sense the shock of the new thing God was doing. If you're sick and unable to sleep much, sometimes the night seems to go on forever. But then, just when you're dozing a bit, suddenly the alarm clock goes off; it really is morning. That's the mood here.

   In what ways are we asleep today in our churches, our communities and our personal lives?

3. To begin his public ministry, Jesus goes to John to be baptized in the Jordan River. What is significant about what happens after his baptism (vv. 9-13)?

4. The whole Christian gospel could be summed up in this point: that when the living God looks at every believing Christian, he says to us what he said to Jesus on that day. He sees us, not as we are in our-

selves, but as we are in Jesus Christ. It sometimes seems impossible, especially to people who have never had this kind of support from their earthly parents, but it's true: God looks at us and says, "You are my dear, dear child; I'm delighted with you."

What would it mean to you to hear God say that to you?

5. When Jesus is sent out into the desert, he is acting out the great drama of Israel's exodus from Egypt, spending forty days in the wilderness instead of forty years.

    Jesus receives affirmation through God's voice from heaven and understands the ultimate reality that God reveals. How would this prepare him for being "in the desert forty days" where "the satan tested him" and he "was with the wild beasts"?

6. *Read Mark 1:14-45.* Jesus begins his ministry by announcing good news. What is that news (vv. 14-15)?

7. Why does Jesus choose to announce that news when John is in prison?

8. If you were to walk down the street of any town or village with any Christian background and were to call out "Repent and believe the gospel," people would think they knew what you meant: "Give up your sins and become a Christian." Of course, Jesus wanted people to stop sinning, but *repentance* for him meant two rather different things as well. First, it meant turning away from the social and political agendas they were trusting in, which were driving Israel into a crazy, ruinous war. Second, it meant calling Israel to turn back to a true loyalty to their God. Jesus' listeners would recognize from the Old Testament prophets that the call to repent is part of the announcement that God's rescue is close at hand.

    To follow Jesus, the fishermen (Peter, Andrew, James and John) have to cut loose from other ties and trust him and his message (vv. 14-20). Why is it often so difficult for us to do likewise today?

9. When Jesus enters the synagogue, he is not one of the recognized teachers, not a priest or scribe or Pharisee who usually taught what "Moses said" or what "Rabbi so-and-so said." How is Jesus' teaching different (vv. 21-22)?

10. How else does Mark say that Jesus demonstrates his authority (vv. 23-34)?

11. Jesus didn't stay in one place like John did. Instead, he traveled around Galilee, preaching the good news and healing many people. But after he heals a leper, why doesn't he want anything to leak out about that healing (vv. 35-45)?

12. In some countries and in certain situations, some Christians will know in prayer that it is better not to attract too much attention to themselves. This isn't cowardice but wisdom. Why might this be the case with Jesus?

13. Looking over this first chapter of Mark, how does Jesus model for us different aspects of announcing the kingdom of God?

PRAY

Offer prayers of thanks and praise to God for Jesus' authority to call his people to his tasks, to expand our view of what God can do and is doing, to teach, to heal, and to defeat the forces of evil.

2

A LIFE OF FORGIVENESS

Mark 2:1—3:6

In many cultures today, forgiveness is seen as a sign of weakness. Revenge, for them, is a moral duty. Sometimes whole families, whole communities, are torn apart this way; think of Northern Ireland, for example. Sometimes whole nations and governments engage in childish, but deadly, tit-for-tat retaliations. People who live that way tend to think that God lives that way too.

We shouldn't be surprised, then, that Jesus' unexpected declaration of forgiveness sent shock waves running through the house, the village, the nation and finally through the world. Forgiveness is the most powerful thing in the world; but because it is so costly, we prefer to settle for second best. Jesus, already on his way to paying the full price, offered nothing less than the best.

OPEN

How has forgiving someone or being forgiven changed you?

STUDY

1. *Read Mark 2:1-22.* How does Jesus respond to the four people making a hole in the roof of his house and letting their paralyzed friend down through it (2:1-12)?

2. What are the different responses to Jesus' offer of forgiveness and healing?

3. The phrase "son of man" that Jesus uses in 2:10 (and later in 2:27) comes from Daniel 7, referring to the representative of God's true people who is opposed by the forces of evil. But God vindicates him, rescues him, proves him to be in the right and gives him authority.

    How does this episode continue and extend the themes of Mark 1?

4. Levi collected taxes for the Roman puppet government the Jews detested so much. He worked for Herod, someone who thought of himself as king of the Jews. So for Jesus to feast with people like Levi—people known locally as "sinners," an easy label to stick on those who didn't conform either to the strict religious requirements of the law or the strict political expectations of opposition to Herod and Rome—was simply outrageous (2:15-17).

So why does Jesus do this?

5. The next event Mark reports deals with fasting, not feasting (2:18-
    22). The main times when Jews of Jesus' day fasted were days that
    reminded them of the great disasters of old, like the time when the
    temple was destroyed by the Babylonians in 587 B.C.

    In response to the people's question about fasting Jesus paints a
    picture of a wedding. The Old Testament, too, used the image of
    God being a bridegroom and Israel being his bride (who was some-
    times rebellious and needed to be wooed back). How is Jesus thus
    responding to the people's challenge?

6. Jesus' ministry often couldn't be fitted into how his fellow Jews
    thought about what God would and should do. How do the two im-
    ages of old and new (2:21-22) communicate about Jesus' kingdom
    ministry?

7. On the one hand Jesus was saying in 1:15 that repentance was needed
    (which at the time was often accompanied by fasting). On the other
    hand he says feasting is appropriate. How do these work together in
    Jesus' announcement of the kingdom?

8. *Read Mark 2:23—3:6.* Because Jesus' teaching was so radical, the Pharisees, who were experts in laws and traditions and sometimes self-appointed guardians of public morality, watched him and his followers. Keeping the sabbath was, of course, one of the Ten Commandments and was one of the things that marked out the Jewish people, over the centuries, from their pagan neighbors—one of the things that reminded them that they were God's people.

   When the Pharisees catch Jesus' disciples illegally plucking corn on the sabbath and confront him about it, what is the significance of Jesus putting himself on par with David in response (2:23-27)?

9. On another sabbath, Jesus heals a man with a withered hand. Why does he perform this healing when he knows people are watching for something to accuse him of (3:1-6)?

10. In what ways is the church today so blinded by a commitment to unnecessary rules that it fails to support God's healing and restorative work?

11. In most of the Western world, society as a whole no longer observes the sabbath as it did in past generations. How can we learn to live in a rhythm of work and rest without becoming legalists in the process?

12. Summarize the main things Jesus has revealed about himself in the episodes found in this section of Mark.

PRAYER

Thank God for who Jesus is and the ways he announces the kingdom to his world.

3

FOLLOWING JESUS

Mark 3:7-35

Wᵃhen I was a boy, the football team I supported, Newcastle United, won the FA Cup, the world's oldest football trophy, three years out of five. Think what it was like in Newcastle when the players came back from the match at Wembley Stadium in London. The whole town turned out to watch and to cheer. Something similar happens when a film or television star comes to town. Or a rock star. Or the president, queen or another ruler. The streets are full of people, trying to get a firsthand look at the famous one; and you wonder where they all came from.

OPEN

Who would you go out of your way to see and why?

STUDY

1. *Read Mark 3:7-19.* Why does Jesus attract huge crowds of followers (vv. 7-12)?

2. Why doesn't he want the unclean spirits to reveal his identity?

3. For what specific purposes does Jesus call twelve of his followers (vv. 13-15)?

4. Every Jew knew that there were twelve tribes in Israel—or, at least, that there had been. What would Jesus, then, be saying about himself and his ministry by choosing twelve to have authority with him in his work?

5. *Read Mark 3:20-35.* As news about Jesus spreads, more people follow him home. What does his family think about him (vv. 20-21)?

6. What do the scribes think about him (v. 22)?

7. What kinds of reactions have you gotten from people when they find out you're a follower of Jesus? If you aren't a follower of Jesus, what is your impression of who he is?

8. How does Jesus answer their accusations (vv. 23-30)?

9. Jesus compares himself to a strong man plundering a house. How does this help us to answer the question about being in league with the devil?

10. When Jesus' family was looking for him (vv. 31-35), how he responded was scandalous. Loyalty to the family was the local and specific outworking of loyalty to Israel as the people of God. But as Mark has already shown us, Jesus was quite capable of challenging the symbols that lay at the heart of the Jewish sense of identity. What does Jesus teach here about family?

11. What allegiances do we hold dear today?

12. How do they sometimes supersede our allegiance to Jesus and his "family"?

13. How can we put our allegiances (whether social, cultural, political, economic or ethnic) back into proper relationship to Jesus?

PRAY

Ask God to help you give priority to Jesus and his family this week.

NOTE ON MARK 3:29

Jesus added a warning which has often been misunderstood. What is this "unforgivable sin" in verse 29? His critics had painted themselves into a corner. Once you label what is in fact the work of the Holy Spirit as the work of the devil, there's no way back. It's like holding a conspiracy theory: all the evidence you see will simply confirm your belief. You will be blind to the truth.

It isn't that God gets specially angry with one sin in particular. It's rather that if you decide firmly that the doctor who is offering to perform a life-saving operation on you is in fact a sadistic murderer, you will never give your consent for the operation. There is no middle way, for the world today as for Israel then. Jesus isn't just a "mildly interesting historical figure," as some in today's world would like him to be. He is either the one who brought God's kingdom or a dangerous madman.

4

PARABLES OF
THE KINGDOM

Mark 4:1-34

I have always enjoyed listening to good choirs. I have even, on rare occasions, sung in one or two, in fear and trembling lest my amateur ability should reveal itself by a wrong note, a fluffed entry or—that dread moment for all irregular singers—keeping the sound going a second too long after everyone else has fallen silent.

When you audition for a choir, often the conductor will ask you to pick a note out of a chord. Here is a chord of three, four or five notes; you can hear it all together, but can you hear the notes individually and sing each in turn? It's often quite a test. Something like that is involved in learning to read Jesus' parables.

OPEN

If you were composing a song about your spiritual life, what would it be like?

STUDY

1. *Read Mark 4:1-20.* This parable is often interpreted as illustrating different ways individuals respond to the gospel, and there is some truth in that, especially as it offers a picture of Jesus' own ministry. Yet, as Jesus and his listeners well knew, the Old Testament frequently uses the image of a vineyard or field or garden to represent Israel, and harvest to represent God's dealings with it (for example, Isaiah 5:1-7; 37:27; Jeremiah 26:18; Ezekiel 16:2, 7).

   If we take this line of thought, what might Jesus be saying about the past, present and future of Israel through this parable?

2. As we have seen in Mark 1—3, Jesus has already attracted a good deal of negative attention.

   He has been challenged by the authorities about forgiving sins, his attitude toward the sabbath and feasting with sinners. His family has said he is out of his mind and the religious leaders have said he is possessed by the devil.

   As we look at Mark 4:11-12 in this context, why might Jesus *not* want some listeners to understand what he is saying?

3. The problem—and this seems to be the main reason Jesus taught in parables—is that Jesus' vision of how God was sowing his word was, as we would say today, politically incorrect. People were expecting a

great moment of renewal. They believed that Israel would be rescued lock, stock and barrel; God's kingdom would explode onto the world stage in a blaze of glory.

How does Jesus' parable offer a different vision of Israel and its future?

4. What preconceptions about how God is supposed to work today might actually prevent us and others from welcoming God and his word?

5. *Read Mark 4:21-34.* What are the promise and the warning found in Mark 4:21-25?

6. How do these carry on themes found in 4:1-20?

7. The traditional translation of verse 25 ("the measure you give will be the measure you get") has inspired all sorts of reflections, including a whole Shakespeare play (*Measure for Measure*), about the meaning of justice. Here Jesus seems to be telling his followers that the level to which they pay attention to what he's teaching them will be the level at which they will receive the benefits of the kingdom.

How can we go more deeply into Jesus' teachings?

8. What's the significance of the farmer sowing seed and not knowing how it grows in relation to the coming of God's kingdom (vv. 26-29)?

9. Though Jesus' ministry in Galilee doesn't look like the sort of kingdom-of-God-movement people were expecting, it was in fact the seedtime for God's long-promised and long-awaited harvest.

When Jesus asks, "What shall we say God's kingdom is like? What picture shall we give of it?" his words echo Isaiah (see Isaiah 40:18). The prophet asked a similar question about God himself: To what will you liken God, or what likeness compare with him?

What aspect of God's kingdom does the mustard seed parable emphasize (vv. 30-32)?

10. Other Old Testament echoes come at the end of the story: the birds of the air make their nests in its shade. Ezekiel and Daniel both use this as an image of a great kingdom, growing like a tree until those around can shelter under it (Ezekiel 17:23; 31:6; Daniel 4:12, 21).

Jesus was happy for people to listen openly and be curious about what he was saying, to have those on the inside ask for more and go more deeply, as is suggested in Mark 4:10-11. Sometimes we feel the pressure to explain the whole gospel all at once to people. How might we instead help them become curious and be motivated to go more deeply into what Jesus is all about?

PRAY

Thank God that you can participate in his kingdom. Then ask him to help you tell others about him and his coming kingdom in such a way that they will want to be part of it too.

TRADING FEAR
FOR FAITH

Mark 4:35—5:43

It isn't only boats that are in danger on the Sea of Galilee. To this day, the parking areas on the western shore have signs warning drivers of what happens in high winds. The sea can get very rough very quickly, and big waves can swamp cars parked on what looked like a safe beach. I have in my study a photograph of the lake, which I took from the top of the Golan Heights on a calm and sunny day; but when the wind suddenly gets up you wouldn't want to hang around outside with a camera. A boat on the lake suddenly gets tossed around like a child's toy. People get tossed around in storms too.

OPEN

How do you normally react to "storms" in your life and why?

STUDY

1. *Read Mark 4:35—5:20.* Mark recorded a time when Jesus and his disciples experienced a rough trip on the Sea of Galilee during a storm. Apart from fishermen, the Jews were not a seafaring people; they left that to their Phoenician neighbors to the north. The sea came to symbolize, for them, the dark power of evil, threatening to destroy God's good creation, God's people, God's purposes.

   What Old Testament character do you recall who slept in a boat in a storm, and yet how does this story in Mark 4:35-41 contrast with that one?

2. Why are the disciples still fearful after Jesus calms the storm (4:41)?

3. Imagine this event as a blockbuster movie—it would need a big screen to do it justice—and you audition for a part. How would you play out your role?

4. From a storm on a lake we shift to a storm within a man. When Jesus and his disciples landed on the southeast shore of the sea, they were in Gentile territory. (Jews don't keep pigs.) A man with an unclean spirit confronted them there. How does Mark describe this Gentile (5:1-6)?

5. How does Jesus deal with him (5:7-20)?

6. Jesus' gentle, healing message is for all Israel and for one Gentile. Why does Jesus tell the man he cannot come with him?

7. *Read Mark 5:21-43.* After healing the demon-possessed man, Jesus crosses the Sea of Galilee again. In the crowd that greets him is Jairus, a synagogue president. What does Jairus do (5:22-23)?

8. Given Jesus' mixed reputation, how might Jairus's actions affect Jairus politically, socially and religiously?

9. While Jesus is walking to Jairus's house, a woman with internal bleeding touches Jesus' clothes (5:25-32). Why does she do that instead of speaking directly to him?

10. As this woman is healed, someone arrives from Jairus's house to tell him his daughter has died. How does Jesus respond to this news (5:35-42)?

11. Why does Jesus command the girl's parents and his companions not to tell anyone about this miracle, whereas he told the demon-possessed man in 5:19 to tell everyone about his healing?

12. Mark places the story of the woman with chronic bleeding inside the story about Jairus's daughter, and obviously means for us to consider them together. How are both stories about fear and faith?

13. When life crowds in with all its storms and pressures, there is still room for us to go directly to Jesus or creep up behind him—if that's all we feel we can do—and reach out to touch him, in that odd mixture of fear and faith that characterizes so much Christian discipleship. What storms and fears of life would you like to bring to the Lord?

PRAY

Thank God that he is more powerful than any storm that comes your way. Ask him to help you reach out to him first when the storms hit.

OPPOSITION MOUNTS

Mark 6:1-29

What sells newspapers? Three things, and if they're combined, so much the better. Royalty: almost any story about a member of a royal family will sell, not only in Britain or Norway or wherever it began, but around the rest of the world. Sex: nothing like a scandal, especially if it's to do with people in high places. Religion: though God has slipped down the ratings in recent years, people are still aware that there are unanswered questions out there, and someone who seems to be an authentic spokesperson for God is newsworthy.

OPEN

If a newspaper reporter were interviewing you, what aspect of your spiritual life might he or she be most interested in and why?

STUDY

1. *Read Mark 6:1-29.* This chapter has it all: royalty, sex and religion. It begins with the latter. When Jesus went back to his home region,

his religious teachings became the center of attraction. But instead of welcoming him, people took offense at him (vv. 1-6). Why?

2. To multiply his ministry, Jesus sends out his twelve disciples in pairs. What is significant about the instructions he gives them (vv. 7-10)?

3. How are they to respond to being unwanted and why (v. 11)?

4. How easy it would be, we naturally think, for knocking the dust off our feet to be an act of pique or petulance. Yet in the context of Jesus' mission, there was no time to waste. The kingdom of God is at hand. Mark's breathless Gospel focuses here on the disciples' breathless mission; and if people won't have it, there's no time to lose. On to the next place, and woe to those who have missed their chance. It was a deeply symbolic act of witness to the Israel of his day as to what time it was in God's urgent timetable.

Part of Christian discipleship is the spiritual sensitivity and discernment to know when there is an emergency on, and what steps to take. There have been many times in recent years, in many places around the globe, when the church's task has been, like the Twelve, to go urgently around, proclaiming and acting out the kingdom.

What situations now need our urgent attention as the church's—as God's—agents of the kingdom?

5. When the king (here's the royalty news) hears about Jesus and what he is doing, some think it is Elijah who, according to Jewish tradition, would return to get things ready for the final judgment (see Malachi 4:5). Why would Herod think Jesus is John the Baptist raised from the dead (vv. 14-16)?

6. Herod had arrested John previously because John opposed Herod's marriage to his brother's wife. (Here's the sex news.) Why did John make such a fuss over this act, especially by one who claimed to be the king of the Jews (vv. 17-18)?

7. Then Herod hosted a birthday bash with scandalous goings-on. And there's nothing private about this story. It would have been round the palace within minutes, round the neighborhood by morning, and round all Galilee within a day or two. If it had happened today it would be all over the newspapers. It's sordid, shabby and shameful—exactly the sort of thing that everybody likes to hear, however much they pretend otherwise.

The worst part of the party was Herod's daughter-in-law—at her mother's suggestion—requesting the head of John the Baptist on a dish. Even though Herod feared and listened to John, why does he order John's beheading (vv. 22-28)?

8. When does the pressure to please people override our desire to obey God?

9. Why does Mark place this story about John the Baptist right after the episode of Jesus sending out the Twelve?

10. What are the costs or potential costs for us as we play our part as agents of God's kingdom?

PRAY

Ask God to give you courage to stand up to opposition and pressure when people don't understand or appreciate your faith.

7

AMAZING COMPASSION

Mark 6:30-56

After a period of exhausting, stressful work, followed by a piece of sudden, devastating news, it would be natural to think that we need a rest, a break, time to recover and regroup. After the disciples return from their mission and hear about John the Baptist being executed, a break is exactly what Jesus seems to have in mind for them. But things don't go as planned.

OPEN

When have important plans you've had been interrupted and how did you respond?

STUDY

1. *Read Mark 6:30-44.* The short boat trip is the only time he and the disciples have to themselves. By the time they get to the shore everyone else has gotten there first.

How does Jesus respond to this interruption of his break?

2. Why do the disciples want to send the people away?

3. What is Jesus' challenge to them instead?

4. How do the disciples respond to this challenge and why?

5. Jesus, however, has compassion and a plan. How does he use the resources they have?

6. When have you seen God use meager resources to meet a challenging situation?

7. How does the leadership (shepherding) Jesus provides contrast with the kind of leader we saw Herod to be in the previous story?

8. What we are seeing here is a sign of *new creation*. Something was going on, there in Jesus' public career, which was unleashing an explosive force into the world. It wasn't what we (or they) would call magic, the manipulation of the natural world to suit one's own ends. It was the power of a totally obedient life, a life given up to the kingdom of God, to God's sovereign and saving rule breaking in at last to a world for so long under enemy occupation. We are probably meant to make the connection between Jesus' compassion for the crowds and his action with the bread and the fish.

    What do you learn about God's coming kingdom from Jesus' actions in this situation?

9. *Read Mark 6:45-56.* It is about 3 a.m. when the disciples see Jesus walking on the sea. What array of emotions do they go through (vv. 49-52)?

10. At this point, within the steady build-up of astonishing events, we hear a dark theme emerge, which is now going to run alongside the other events until it achieves an initial response in chapter 8. "They hadn't understood about the loaves," says Mark of the disciples, "because their hearts were hardened." It's the first time he's said some-

thing like that about the disciples, but we haven't heard the last of it by any means.

What have the disciples not understood about the loaves that they should have?

11. What causes our hearts to be hardened?

12. Notice that this chapter closes with a rerun of events. People were drawn to Jesus for healing, and he didn't turn them away even though that wasn't his primary reason for being there. How can you show compassion and help others even when people interrupt your plans?

PRAY

Ask God for a heart of compassion for others especially when they interrupt our plans.

8

THE HEART
OF THE MATTER

Mark 7:1-37

All societies have purity laws of one sort or another. Children in the Western world today are taught quite strictly when and how to wash their hands to prevent infection and disease. And woe betide any restaurant owner or delicatessen manager whose staff don't observe a very strict code of hygiene. They could very well be shut down for various violations. Even fancy cruise ships are known sometimes to struggle with germs that can make most of the passengers and crew very sick. Hospitals, which of course intentionally bring in sick people to heal them, also often have very difficult times keeping one patient from being infected by another.

Israel in Jesus' day had its own set of purity laws as well. Ritual washing of hands before food, and of cooking vessels, was one key part of a highly complex and developed system of purity regulations. These were eventually codified and written down about two hundred years after Jesus' day, but they were already well known, in the form of oral traditions, by his time.

OPEN

What were you taught about cleanliness when you were growing up?

STUDY

1. *Read Mark 7:1-23.* Suddenly Mark's stories about healing have stopped for a minute, and we have a debate instead, focusing on a controversy about the interpretation and practice of Judaism by Jesus and his followers.

   What is the problem according to the Pharisees (vv. 1-5)?

2. What is the problem according to Jesus, and how does he illustrate it (vv. 6-13)?

3. Are there ways that your church or fellowship gives verbal assent to something in Scripture but doesn't always live by it? If so, what are they?

4. Some of the most famous martyr stories in Jesus' world were about Jewish people who had been tortured and killed for refusing to eat unclean food, particularly pork. And Jesus has grasped something, a deep truth about the way humans are and about what God is now up to, which means that as part of his kingdom-message he must take a different line.

   In Mark 7:14-23, what is radically different about Jesus' teaching on what is clean and unclean?

5. At first glance it might look like Jesus is saying in 7:14-23 that external and physical things are irrelevant or bad and that internal or spiritual things are good. What is he saying instead?

6. In 7:1-23 how does Jesus say both that sometimes people don't take Scripture seriously enough and that sometimes they take it too far?

7. In question 3 we considered ways in which people don't take Scripture seriously enough. What might be ways people today take Scripture too far?

8. *Read Mark 7:24-37.* Jesus knew that God's blessing to all the nations would come through Israel (see Genesis 12:1-3; Matthew 10:5-6; and Romans 15:8-9). After Israel was redeemed, the rest of the world would also receive God's saving blessing. Here he offers an early signal of what lies ahead.

   Why does Jesus finally respond positively to the request of this Gentile woman whose daughter had an unclean spirit (vv. 24-30)?

9. How does Jesus affirm in this episode the same point about cleanness and uncleanness that he made in 7:1-23?

10. Although Jesus healed the deaf mute, he wanted to keep some things secret until the right moment. But the news didn't just leak out—it poured out, as people simply couldn't stop talking about what they'd seen him do. But this is a puzzle. Why would Jesus do things like this if he didn't want people to talk about them (vv. 31-36)?

11. Jewish people in Jesus' day are not the only ones who let traditions that maintain their identity get in the way of other people experiencing a right relationship with God. How might you and your congregation do the same thing today?

12. What is one change you need to make in your everyday life, so traditions you keep don't turn people away from God?

PRAY

Ask God to examine your heart and show you your motivations for right living. Confess any motivations that come from wanting to look good or keep traditions that are contrary to scriptural teaching—and that tend to keep people away from God. Then pray for the discernment to know which traditions are in line with Scripture and which are not.

NOTE ON MARK 7:24-30

The story of the Syrophoenician woman, especially where Jesus implies that she and Gentiles in general are "dogs" (v. 27), is now regularly made the basis of a fashionable theory concerning Jesus' innate prejudices. This is not the only way to read the story as Caird and Hurst's *New Testament Theology* (p. 395) makes clear:

> Apart from the obvious danger of building an entire reconstruction on one reported incident, one must be especially aware of the problem incurred by the loss of *tone* in any reported saying of Jesus. . . . Jesus' words, which in cold print seem so austere, were almost certainly spoken with a smile and a tone of voice which invited the woman's witty reply. Jesus must have been aware of the prejudice against Gentiles which existed among many of his contemporaries, and in view of the use of irony found elsewhere in his teaching, it would be surprising not to find a vestige of it in this.

Bailey in *Jesus Through Middle Eastern Eyes* (pp. 223ff.) suggests that Jesus takes the narrow-minded attitudes of his disciples and presses them to their logical extreme. As Bailey says, "The verbalization is authentic to their [the disciples'] attitudes and feelings, but shocking when put into words and thrown in the face of a desperate, kneeling woman pleading for the sanity of her daughter. It is acutely embarrassing to hear and see one's deepest prejudices verbalized and demonstrated." Jesus ultimately not only honors the woman as one of the few who "bests" him in an argument but also teaches his disciples a lesson regarding their mistaken ideas about the kingdom.

9

FAILING THE TEST

Mark 8:1—9:1

Think of your school days. What was your worst subject—the one you always dreaded, the one you longed to give up? Now try (if the memory isn't too painful) to remember what it was like sitting in a desk with the teacher trying to explain something to you for the twentieth or thirtieth time. Teachers have a particular type of sorrowful look when they have said something as clearly as they can, over and over again, and the pupil still doesn't get it.

OPEN

If you have ever been a teacher, whether in a school, in a church ministry or as a parent, how did you feel when your students or children didn't understand what you were teaching?

Or if you've never taught, how did you feel when you didn't understand something a teacher tried to explain to you?

STUDY

1. *Read Mark 8:1-21.* As a teacher, I think Jesus had that sorrowful look

on his face more than once during the events recorded in this passage. What's more, he knew it was important that the disciples learn the lessons sooner rather than later.

How is this feeding of a crowd (8:1-10) different from the feeding of the five thousand recorded in Mark 6:30-44?

2. What can we learn today from this strange story and its earlier look-alike companion?

3. It is noticeable that in both stories Jesus not only feeds the crowds; he involves his disciples in the feeding. The closer we are to Jesus, the more likely it is that he will call us to share in his work of compassion, healing and feeding, bringing his kingdom-work to an ever wider circle. The Christian life, as a disciplined rhythm of following Jesus, involves not only being fed but becoming, in turn, one through whom Jesus' love can be extended to the world.

After this act of compassion, things get hotter. Right on cue, the Pharisees appear (8:11). What is ironic about them asking for a sign just at this point in the story?

4. Instead of giving them a sign, Jesus and his disciples got in a boat to cross the water. He warned them against the "leaven" of the Pharisees and of Herod. The Jews used leaven to make ordinary bread,

but at Passover time they were forbidden it, to remind them of when they were in such a hurry to leave their slavery in Egypt that they only had time to make unleavened bread.

In light of what you've learned from Mark so far, why does Jesus give this warning (8:14-21)?

5. In the middle of it all, Jesus quotes from the prophet Jeremiah (5:21). This isn't just a poetic way of saying "I can't believe how blind you are." It's a way of saying "You're in danger of going the way of the Israelites in Jeremiah's day!" People were so caught up with their own concerns, and so unconcerned about injustice and wickedness in their society, that God had no alternative but to abandon them to their fate at the hands of foreigners. If they effectively worship other gods, those other gods (and their devotees) will have power over them.

In what ways are the disciples like the people in Jeremiah's day?

6. The confrontation between Jesus' kingdom-mission and its rivals is coming up fast. He is anxious that the disciples should understand what's happening. He wants us to do the same today.

What would make Jesus groan today? What is it about us that would make him say, like a frustrated teacher, "You still don't get it"?

7. *Read Mark 8:22—9:1.* When they arrive in Bethsaida, Jesus heals an-
    other blind man (8:22-26). How is this healing related to what hap-
    pened in the boat?

8. The blind man needs two touches to bring his physical sight. What
    two touches did the disciples need to bring the spiritual sight Peter
    articulates in 8:27-30?

9. The Jewish people were expecting a Messiah they thought would
    be God's agent in bringing in the kingdom, in sorting out the mess
    and muddle Israel was in politically, in putting the Gentiles in their
    place. Peter's reaction makes it clear that's the way he thought.

    How does Jesus redefine what the Messiah would do instead here in
    8:31—9:1 and throughout the first eight chapters of Mark?

10. Jesus asks us the same question he asked his disciples: "Who do you
    say I am?" What is your answer to who Jesus is and what he is actu-
    ally doing in the world?

11. The disciples must have known that by following Jesus they were
    taking risks. The death of Jesus' mentor, John the Baptist, will simply

have confirmed that. But now Jesus began to teach them something new, implying that once they'd declared that he was the Messiah, they'd need to pick up their own cross (8:34). How can following Jesus be dangerous for us as well?

12. This passage makes it clear that following Jesus is the only way to go. Following Jesus is, more or less, Mark's definition of what being a Christian means; and Jesus is not leading us on a pleasant afternoon hike, but on a walk into danger and risk.

How have you seen in your life and in others' lives the truth that "if you want to save your life, you'll lose it; but if you lose your life because of me and the Message you'll save it"?

PRAY

Ask God for quick understanding of the lessons he is trying to teach you and for strength to follow him even when there are obstacles to doing so.

FAITH GETS DIFFICULT

Mark 9:2-29

Science teachers never tire, so I'm told, of the moment when a child first looks into a microscope. What up until then had seemed a boring little speck of dirt can suddenly become full of pattern, color and interest. The child will never look at things the same way again; everything now has the potential to be more than it seems.

The same thing happens elsewhere. Telescopes transform the night sky into a world of awe and power. A good actor can turn an apparently insignificant line into a profound and moving statement of beauty and truth.

OPEN

Describe a time when you discovered something new in a common experience and how it affected you.

STUDY

1. *Read Mark 9:2-29.* Take these quite common experiences and move them up a few notches on the scale of fact and experience. The story

of Jesus' "transformation" or "transfiguration" (vv. 2-13) describes what seems to have been an actual event, but an event in which the deepest significance of everyday reality suddenly and overwhelmingly confronted Peter, James and John.

It's easy enough (and the three of them must have known this) to dismiss such an experience as a hallucination, albeit a very odd one. The three watchers were of course terrified, and Peter blurts out the first thing that comes into his head. The sheer oddity of his bumbling suggestion is itself strong evidence of the story's basic truth. Nobody inventing a tale like this would make up such a comic moment, lowering the tone of the occasion in such a fashion.

How have we so far seen in Mark's Gospel Jesus continuing and finishing the work of Moses and Elijah?

2. As at Jesus' baptism (1:9-11), a voice from the sky speaks, affirming Jesus as the deeply loved Son we should listen to.

   How can we listen more closely to Jesus' voice?

3. The disciples were puzzled about what Jesus meant by "rising from the dead" (vv. 9-10). In Jewish thought in Jesus' day, "the resurrection" would happen to all the righteous at the end of time, not to one person ahead of all the others. They couldn't understand Jesus' implication that the Son of Man would rise from the dead, while they would be still living the sort of normal life in which people would tell one another what they had seen months and years before.

Jewish tradition held that Elijah would return before the final victory of God's people (see Malachi 4:5). In the next exchange about Elijah (vv. 11-13), what is Jesus talking about when he says Elijah has already come?

4. At Caesarea Philippi he had told his followers that it was time to take up the cross. His vocation, and the disciples' awareness of it, has been confirmed by the heavenly voice. The road now leads to Jerusalem.

   It begins with a problem for the disciples. What is that problem (vv. 14-18)?

5. How do the father's words in 9:24 echo your own feelings at times?

6. How does Jesus deal with the problem (vv. 19-27)?

7. The disciples have turned a corner in their pilgrimage; now it's getting harder. People today often suppose that the early years of a person's Christian pilgrimage are the difficult ones, and that as you go on in the Christian life it gets more straightforward. The opposite is frequently the case. Precisely when you learn to walk beside Jesus,

you are given harder tasks, which will demand more courage, more spiritual energy.

How have you seen this truth in your life?

8. What have you learned from this passage about what to do when you face problems and crises?

PRAY

Thank God that he will help you even when you have doubts instead of complete faith, especially when you face problems and crises. Ask him to help you turn to him anyway and believe he will act.

11

WELCOME TO THE WAR

Mark 9:30-50

During the Second World War, while London was being heavily bombed, one of the canons of Westminster Abbey watched as his house, and everything in it, went up in flames after a direct hit. The clothes he stood up in were all he had left. In the morning, he went to Oxford to visit a friend and, while there, went to a shop to buy some new clothes.

The shop assistant was surprised by all the things he was asking for. "Don't you know there's a war on?" she asked. Of course he did, and that's the point of the story.

We, too, are engaged in war, although it's different from this one. The disciples were similarly in a battle—but what Jesus now says to them implies that they don't know. There is a serious business afoot, which will have serious consequences; and unless they realize this they will be in real danger.

OPEN

How and why does a battle suddenly make differences of class or race or opinion among soldiers irrelevant?

STUDY

1. *Read Mark 9:30-37.* What does Jesus teach his disciples about coming events?

2. Why don't the disciples want to understand the plain meaning of what Jesus is telling them?

Earlier in the Gospel, Jesus said things to them in code, and they didn't get it. They have struggled to get their minds round the fact that he often says things that have a clear meaning at the surface level, but what he wants is for them to look under the surface and find a hidden meaning somewhere else. And now he tells them something which we, the readers, realize he means quite literally; and they, not surprisingly, are puzzled because they are looking for a hidden meaning and can't find it.

3. When and why are we like the disciples in this situation—sometimes failing to hear (meaning listen and obey) something from Scripture or something from church or something in prayer?

4. What is on the disciples' minds as they travel to Capernaum that is preventing them from understanding Jesus (vv. 33-34)?

5. What does this argument tell us about their understanding of Jesus and his mission?

6. How does Jesus define greatness (vv. 35-37)?

7. How does his attitude toward children illustrate his point about greatness?

8. How do our concerns for status in the Christian community sometimes get in our way of both understanding Jesus and participating in his mission?

9. *Read Mark 9:38-50.* How does Jesus' attitude toward the man casting out demons in Jesus' name differ from the disciples' attitude?

10. How is the disciples' attitude similar to how Christians react today toward other Christians who aren't part of "our" group?

11. Virtually all readers agree that Jesus' commands in 9:42-48 are not to be taken literally. What does Jesus teach about discipleship with his use of these graphic pictures?

There's a war on. God is at work in our world; so are the forces of evil; and there really is no time or space for self-indulgent spiritualities that shirk the slightest personal cost, or even resist it on the grounds that all the desires and hopes one finds within one's heart must be God-given and so must be realized.

Gehenna, the word in this passage that some translations render as "hell," is the valley that runs past the southwest corner of the old city of Jerusalem. In ancient times it was Jerusalem's rubbish heap, smoldering perpetually; by Jesus' day it had already become a metaphor for the fate, after death, of those who reject God's way.

12. How does Jesus' final command in verse 50 tie back to the issues raised in verses 33-34 and 38?

13. In what ways do you and those in your Christian community need to be at peace with each other?

PRAY

Thank God that you are not alone in these spiritual battles. Ask for his strength to fight against sin instead of giving in to it.

RETHINKING
CONTROVERSIAL ISSUES

Mark 10:1-31

In Britain during the early 1990s, from time to time a journalist would telephone a bishop or theologian to ask about divorce. It happened to me once. It's a question every church, every member of the clergy, has to think about at some time today, especially in the Western world. A newspaper article on divorce will be widely read. Everybody knows someone who is going through, or has just gone through, the breakup of a marriage.

But of course the journalists weren't wanting to write a piece about the church's attitude to divorce in general. They were wanting to write about Prince Charles and Princess Diana. Once it became clear that their marriage was in real trouble, the journalists never left it alone for a minute. Anyone trying to pronounce on the broader question of divorce would at once be seized on: "Are you then saying that Prince Charles . . ." Something very similar was happening when the Pharisees asked Jesus about divorce, because everybody knew that Herod Antipas, the ruling king, had taken his brother's wife.

OPEN

What are some controversial areas Christians deal with today?

STUDY

1. *Read Mark 10:1-16.* Divorce and remarriage is as much a controversial issue for Christians today as it was for the Pharisees who asked Jesus about it. Remembering Herod's marital status from Mark 6 and what happened to John the Baptist, how could the Pharisees' question put Jesus in a tough spot no matter how he answered?

2. How does Jesus deal with this trap?

3. In this dialogue what point is Jesus making by going to what Moses *commanded* about divorce in Genesis 1:27 and 2:24 while the Pharisees note instead what Moses *permitted* about divorce in Deuteronomy 24:1-4?

4. When Jesus is safely back in the privacy of the house with his disciples, what does Jesus add to his answer (vv. 10-12)?

The problem, Jesus says, was not with the ideal, nor with the law, but with the people: Israel was, when it all came down to it, just like everybody else. Hardhearted. Eager to take the precious gift of genuine humanness and exploit or abuse it. This means that, for Jesus' comment to make sense, *he must be offering a cure for hardheartedness:* the coming of the kingdom.

5. How does Jesus' attitude toward children differ from that of his disciples (vv. 13-16)?

6. What characteristic of a child do you want to emulate in your relationship with God?

7. How are these discussions about divorce and about children connected?

8. *Read Mark 10:17-31.* What is the rich man looking for (v. 17)?

9. Jesus answers his question by restating the basic commandments that every Jewish person knew well; we call them the Ten Commandments. What is the focus of the ones he quotes (v. 19)?

10. Look at the Ten Commandments found in Exodus 20:1-17. How do the commandments Jesus leaves out in 10:19 relate to his directive in verse 21?

11. Many first-century Jews divided the time into the *present age* and the *age to come*. The present age, their own time, was full of sin and injustice, lying and oppression. Good people suffered; wicked people got away with it. But in the age to come that would all be different.

    Why are the disciples shocked that wealth won't buy a place in the age to come (vv. 23-26)?

    Jesus says riches can no more go into the age to come than a camel can go through a needle—a typical and deliberate Middle-Eastern overstatement. It's like saying, "You'll get your riches into God's kingdom when you can put the entire ocean into a bottle."

12. Many today (just as was common in both Judaism and paganism of

Jesus' day) thought wealth was a sign of God's pleasure. How can wealth actually be a hindrance to us in our call to follow Jesus?

13. In what area is Jesus asking you to change your thinking or your actions as you follow him?

PRAY

Ask God to help you understand his teaching on controversial issues you encounter this week, then to obey him.

13

NOT WHAT YOU EXPECT

Mark 10:32-52

What comes to mind first when you think of the crucifixion of Jesus?

Perhaps you think of going to church and singing well-known hymns: "There is a green hill far away," or "When I survey the wondrous cross."

Perhaps you think of a picture, or a statue, of the cross: a crucifix, reminding you of the sorrow and suffering of Jesus, and somehow bringing consolation and hope into your own sorrow and suffering.

Perhaps you think of the brutality that could have dreamed up that way of killing people—and of the similar brutalities that still deface God's world today.

Perhaps you have an image in your mind of the crowds at the foot of the cross, some mocking Jesus, some in tears. Perhaps, in your picture, you are there with them, watching him die.

OPEN

What pictures come to mind when you think of Jesus' crucifixion, and how does that affect you?

STUDY

1. *Read Mark 10:32-45.* Mark is going to tell us the story of how Jesus was crucified. And he wants us to hold in our minds several pictures which will give us the full meaning of the scene, for Jesus, for Israel, for the world and for ourselves. In this passage he wants, as it were, to sow the seeds of these different pictures. These seeds will germinate during the next few chapters.

    What events does Jesus say will occur after they arrive in Jerusalem (vv. 32-34)?

2. What do James and John request of Jesus?

3. What does this request reveal about how they view this journey?

4. The cross isn't just about God forgiving our sins because of Jesus' death (though of course this is central to it). Because it is God's way of putting the world, and ourselves, right, it challenges and subverts all the human systems which claim to put the world right but in fact only succeed in bringing a different set of humans out on top. The reason James and John misunderstand Jesus is exactly the same as the reason why many subsequent thinkers, down to our own day, are desperate to find a way of having Jesus without having the cross as well: the cross calls into question all human pride and glory.

What does Jesus' response to their request teach about following him (vv. 38-45)?

5. What is unexpected about Jesus' teaching about leadership and discipleship?

6. How can Jesus' teaching about leadership guide you or leaders in your Christian community?

James and John don't know what they're asking for, but Mark's reader, after a few chapters of waiting in suspense, will discover it. When Jesus "sits in his glory," with one at his right and another at his left, it will be on the cross. Mark has given us a stark picture both of what true kingly glory looks like (v. 45) and of what Jesus' death will mean.

7. *Read Mark 10:46-52.* On the way to Jerusalem, Jesus and his disciples come to Jericho, where Bartimaeus, a blind beggar, shouts at them. What does Bartimaeus want from Jesus?

8. This is the kind of story that lends itself particularly well to meditation. Imagine yourself in the crowd that day in Jericho. It's hot,

dry and dusty. You're excited; you're with Jesus; you're going up to Jerusalem. And here is someone shouting from the roadside. It's a nuisance. It's possibly even dangerous (if enough people call him "Son of David," someone in authority is going to get alarmed).

When have you felt like the disciples do in this passage?

9. What does Jesus mean by the question he asks Bartimaeus in return (vv. 49-52)?

10. How do Bartimaeus's actions stand in contrast to the disciples' in the last couple chapters?

When Jesus says "Your faith has saved you," the word *saved* refers once again to physical healing. For any early Christian, though, it would carry a wider and deeper meaning as well. The different dimensions of salvation were not sharply distinguished either by Jesus or by the Gospel writers. God's rescue of people from what we think of as physical ailments on the one hand and spiritual peril on the other were thought of as different aspects of the same event. But again not for the first time, we see that the key to salvation, of whatever kind, is faith. That's why anyone, even those normally excluded from pure or polite society, can be saved. Faith is open to all; and often it's the unexpected people who seem to have it most strongly. And faith consists not least in recognizing who Jesus is and trusting that he has the power to rescue.

11. Imagine yourself as the blind man. We all have something, by no means necessarily a physical ailment, that we know is getting in the way of our being the people we believe God wants us to be and made us to be. What is it you want Jesus to do for you?

PRAY

Ask for openness and faith to ask for and receive what you want Jesus to do for you.

14

JESUS IN JERUSALEM

Mark 11:1-33

If you've ever been to the Holy Land, you will know that to go from Jericho to Jerusalem involves a long, hard climb. Jericho is the lowest city on earth, over 800 feet below sea level. Jerusalem, which is only a dozen or so miles away, is nearly 3,000 feet *above* sea level. The road goes through hot, dry desert all the way to the top of the Mount of Olives at which point, quite suddenly, you have at the same time the first real vegetation and the first, glorious sight of Jerusalem itself. Even if you were climbing that road every week on business, there would still be a sense of exhilaration, of delight and relief, when you got to the top.

Now add to that sense of excitement the feeling that Jewish pilgrims, coming south from Galilee, would have every time they went up to Jerusalem for a festival (as they did several times a year). They were coming to the place where the living God had chosen to place his name and his presence; the place where, through the regular daily sacrifices, he assured Israel of forgiveness, of fellowship with himself, of hope for their future.

OPEN

Describe something you've done or a place you've visited that gave you a sense of excitement. Why did it affect you that way?

STUDY

1. *Read Mark 11:1-11.* It was Passover time—freedom time! But it was also, as far as they were concerned, kingdom time: the time when Passover dreams, the great hope of freedom, of God's sovereign and saving presence being revealed in a quite new way, would at last come true.

   Jesus riding over the Mount of Olives, across the Kidron Valley, up to the temple mount would clearly have called to mind words of the prophet Zechariah for those watching. What do Zechariah 9:9-10 and 14:4 indicate Jesus is saying about himself?

2. How does the reaction of the people confirm that they understand Jesus' symbolic message?

3. "Hosannah" is a Hebrew word which mixes exuberant praise to God with the prayer that God will save his people, and do so right away. The beginning and end of their cheerful chant is taken from Psalm 118:25-26, which is itself all about going up to Jerusalem and the temple. The sentence that follows means, literally, "Blessed is the one who comes"; but in Hebrew and Aramaic that's the way you say "welcome." In the middle of the chant they have inserted the dangerous prayer: Welcome to the kingdom of our father David!

   You don't spread cloaks on the road for friends or even for family—especially in the Middle East, dusty and stony as it was. But you do it for royalty. How does Jesus' kingship call us to put our property at his disposal?

4. Why would Mark bother to mention that Jesus looked around the temple and left (v. 11)?

5. *Read Mark 11:12-33.* In verses 12-14, why does Jesus apparently condemn the fig tree?

6. How different is the temple here from what it was supposed to be (vv. 15-17)?

7. How do the religious leaders react to Jesus' actions and teaching (v. 18)?

8. Mark has given us the story, once again, in "sandwich" form. The outer part concerns the fig tree, the inner part concerns the temple.

   Jesus and his listeners would recall that in Jeremiah 8:11-13 and

24:1-10 God uses figs to depict judgment on Israel and its leaders. We should also keep in mind that "this mountain" (v. 22), in context, almost certainly refers to the temple mountain Jesus and the disciples have just descended.

How then do both parts of this "sandwich" of the fig tree and the temple help explain each other?

9. In encouraging his followers to pray with confident boldness for the present order to be replaced by God's new order, Jesus is quite clear that there can be no personal malice or aggression involved in such work. Even at the very moment where Jesus is denouncing the system that had so deeply corrupted God's intention for Israel, his final word is the stern command to forgive. Perhaps only those who have learned what that means will be in a position to act with Jesus' authority against the injustice and wickedness of our own day.

Why is it often difficult for us to hold together both a deep desire for God's will to be done on earth and a spirit of peace and forgiveness?

10. When the religious leaders ask Jesus about his authority, he counters with his own question. Why can't the chief priests answer Jesus' question (vv. 27-33)?

11. The question of Jesus' authority has come full circle. In the early chapters of the Gospel this was the thing that most impressed people in Galilee (1:22, 27; 2:10; 3:15). Now the authority with which he taught and healed was turned into explicit authority over the highest institution within Judaism. Who did he think he was? From here there is a straight line to the questions before the chief priest after Jesus' arrest (14:55-64). The incident in the temple is the key to the unfolding drama.

If we take the New Testament seriously, it appears that those who follow Jesus, who are equipped with his Spirit, are themselves given authority, under his direction, to act in his name in the world. How can we do so today?

PRAY

Ask God to show you one way to act in his name in your spheres of influence this week and to give you courage to do so.

TRAGEDY AND TRAPS

Mark 12:1-44

What if you had to deliver bad news? And suppose you had to deliver it to the rulers of your country? And suppose the bad news wasn't about a natural disaster or problems with the economy or a scandal in government or a war that was going badly? What if the bad news was that the leaders, the very people you were talking to, were the problem? Their policies were wrong. They were blind to reality. They were headed for disaster.

You may say that's a lot of supposing. But unless we imagine ourselves in something like the situation Jesus faced, we will never understand passages like we find in Mark 12.

OPEN

When have you received bad news? What helped and what didn't help in the way it was given?

STUDY

1. *Read Mark 12:1-12.* Who do the different characters in this parable represent?

2. How do the religious leaders react to this parable?

3. This parable didn't need an explanation. No going back into the house to tell the disciples what it was all about; everybody could tell right away. This was partly because Jesus was adapting a well-known story in Isaiah 5 that compares Israel to a vineyard. There is no happy ending to this story. As it stands, it is pure tragedy. All that is left is judgment. It's a terrifying picture of what happens if the people of God persistently reject the purpose for which God has called them.

   In verses 10-11 Jesus goes on to quote from Psalm 118, the same psalm that excited worshipers were using when singing their hosannas a few days before (see Mark 11:9). What is Jesus saying with this quotation?

4. *Read Mark 12:13-27.* Regarding the question the Pharisees and Herodians ask, how could Jesus equally get in trouble (but with different groups) by saying, "Pay taxes," or by saying, "Don't pay taxes" (vv. 13-15)?

5. How does Jesus avoid being trapped (vv. 15-17)?

6. This passage isn't designed as a full-scale statement of Christian truth on "religion and society" or "church and state." It was a quick and sharp-edged quip for a particular occasion. You can't divide human life, and the world, into two segments. That's a much later idea, which gained ground only in the eighteenth century. Jewish thought at the time, and Christian thought as it emerged within Judaism, has always seen the entire world and everything in it as created by the one God. All aspects of it fall under his sovereign and saving rule.

   What aspects of life today are people tempted to believe are separate from religious conviction or don't have much if anything to do with faith?

7. A different group of religious leaders, the Sadducees, try another trap with Jesus by telling him a (presumably hypothetical) story, which depended on an ancient Jewish law (found in Deuteronomy 25:5-10 and Genesis 38:8). What is the trap this time (vv. 18-23)?

8. How does Jesus turn this trap around (vv. 24-27)?

The whole point of the Jewish doctrine of resurrection was that it meant a new embodied life, a life that would be given at some future date, *after* whatever sort of "life after death" God's people were enjoying. Resurrection will not simply reproduce every aspect of our present humanity. It will be a recognizable and reembodied human existence; but a great change will have taken place as well, whose precise nature we can at present only guess at.

9. *Read Mark 12:28-44.* After the two traps religious leaders set and failed at, a lawyer approaches Jesus with another question. What does he want to know and how does Jesus answer him?

10. Jesus commends the lawyer for understanding that following these two commandments is worth more "than all burnt offerings and sacrifices" (vv. 32-34). When many Christians have very strong ideas about what worship should and shouldn't be like, how does this passage reveal that we sometimes have misplaced priorities?

At one level, this passage enables us to understand more fully what Jesus thought his work was all about, and how his overall mission was bound to challenge the centrality of the temple and its sacrificial system—a highly controversial, not to say dangerous, thing to suggest. Jesus really did believe that through his kingdom-mission Israel's God would enable people to worship and love him, and to love one another, in a new way, the way promised in the prophets, the way that stemmed from renewed hearts and lives. At another level, this comes as a considerable challenge to all contemporary

Christians, asking if our concern for our neighbor really exceeds our concern for what happens in church on a Sunday morning.

11. The question of messiahship has been swirling all around Mark's Gospel. It was commonly understood from the Old Testament that the Messiah would come from David's line. Now Jesus offers a riddle of his own in verses 35-37. How does Jesus expand their ideas about the Messiah?

12. Jesus commends the widow who gave what seemed to be a very small amount. How does the widow's offering foreshadow Jesus' own coming sacrifice?

13. The great commandments call us to love God "with all your heart, and with all your soul, and with all your understanding, and with all your strength" and to "love your neighbor as yourself." Jesus underscored this with his teaching about paying taxes and about the giving of a poor widow. What is he teaching you?

PRAY

Ask God to show you ways to love him "with all your heart, and with all your soul, and with all your understanding, and with all your strength" and to "love your neighbor as yourself."

NOTE ON MARK 12:25

Some people, even lifelong Christians, assume that when we die we become angels. There is no warrant for this in the Bible. Such notions are a kind of folk religion. But Mark 12:25 is about as close as the Bible gets to suggesting that humans become angels. So what did Jesus mean?

He did not say we would be like angels in every respect. We will be like angels only in that we will not marry and have offspring.

The misunderstanding of Jesus here comes from our common misunderstanding of what resurrection itself is. What Jesus and his contemporaries meant by *resurrection* was not resuscitation, coming back into exactly the same sort of physical life as before. Rather *resurrection* meant and means "transformation" into a new sort of bodily life.

Neither does *resurrection* mean simply "life after death," which many imagine takes place in a disembodied state called heaven where, among other things, angels may be found. Though we may experience such a state for a period of time, that is not the final, eternal condition the Bible teaches. Rather it is a *"life after* life after death"—a reembodied human existence but with a great change that will take place, the precise nature we can only guess at, though Jesus' own resurrection body no doubt gives us some clue.

16

SIGNS OF THE END

Mark 13:1-37

In the everyday world of the ancient Middle East, a good deal of intimate family life goes on in a semipublic world where everyone knows everyone else's business. From childhood people would be well aware of the agonies that take place for a woman giving birth.

The picture of birth pangs had been used for centuries by Jews as they reflected on the way in which, as they believed, their God was intending to bring to birth his new world, his new creation, the age to come in which justice and peace, mercy and truth would at last flourish. From the great prophets onwards they spoke of the world going through the labor pains that would herald the birth of the new day. Many writers from Jesus' time whose works have come down to us spoke of the Jewish hope in this fashion.

Since, as we have already seen, Jesus believed that his kingdom-mission, his message, was the divinely appointed means of bringing this new world to birth, we shouldn't be surprised that he sometimes spoke of it in this way as well.

OPEN

What examples can you think of in which something new and important happened after a period of significant struggle?

STUDY

1. *Read Mark 13:1-27.* In chapters 11 and 12, Jesus has symbolically enacted judgment on the temple (with the money changers in the temple itself and on the fig tree), claimed authority over the temple, judged the leaders of the temple and affirmed that the two great commandments are much more important than sacrifices in the temple.

   How do the opening verses of chapter 13 indicate that the disciples still haven't understood what he's saying?

2. Herod's temple, though still incomplete in Jesus' day, had the reputation of being the most beautiful building in the whole world, and was certainly the largest and most imposing structure for hundreds of miles in any direction. The disciples are astonished at Jesus' prediction and naturally want to know when it will happen.

   Many people have read Mark 13 as being mainly about "the end of the world," which it certainly isn't. Jesus is focused (as is the disciples' question) on the temple's destruction. (If it were the end of the world, what would be the point of running away to the mountains as verse 14 suggests?) Jesus draws on the cosmic language of the Old Testament, as the prophets themselves often did, to indicate the world-changing nature of events that would transpire for Israel. For most Jews at the time, it would indeed be the equivalent of the end of the world for the temple (the center of their national life and identity) to be destroyed.

   How does Jesus say his followers should act as they live through events that will lead up to the destruction of the temple (vv. 5-13)?

3. Jesus' warnings to his followers are to be taken very seriously by all who are called to work for the kingdom today. Many Christians today face persecution every bit as severe as that which the early church suffered; and those Christians who don't face persecution often face the opposite temptation, to stagnate, to become cynical, to suppose that nothing much is happening, that the kingdom of God is just a pious dream.

In verse 13 Jesus says we need patience to hold onto our faith in the midst of difficulties. What specific situation in your life right now do you need patience for?

4. How can we cultivate deeper patience in our lives?

5. After the period of patience Jesus describes, what does he say will happen next (vv. 14-27)?

6. While Jesus encourages patience during the preliminary events leading up to the temple's destruction, one particular sign will indicate that things have changed dramatically and that it is now time to run. The sign is "the desolating abomination" (v. 14), an appalling object or person (Jesus is not exactly clear which) whose presence signifies imminent destruction. The text behind this is Daniel 11:31 and 12:11, which speaks of pagan armies invading Jerusalem, stopping the regular sacrifices in the temple and setting up what sounds

like a pagan idol. When something like that happens, patience is not the proper response. Rather it is escape.

Indeed that is exactly what happened in A.D. 70, within a generation, as Jesus predicted (see v. 30). The Romans conducted a siege of Jerusalem with terrible consequences for the population. Ultimately they set up their own symbols of power and authority in the temple before destroying it. The first-century historian Josephus tells us of many would-be messiahs, many prophets, during the Roman-Jewish war of A.D. 66-70. They were offering rescue, trying to gain a following, promising signs and wonders. They all came to nothing.

Clearly the fulfillment of such a prophecy would have supported Jesus' status as prophet. How does it also show the futility of trusting in the temple and all it stood for as the Jewish leaders of Jesus' day did?

7. The temple, while a symbol of Jewish identity and nationhood, by virtue of that intense focus, prevented Jews from liberally making God's blessing available to those who weren't Jews. How can focusing on our own identity actually prevent us from freely offering God's blessing to those who aren't like us or in our group?

8. *Read Mark 13:28-37.* What warnings and admonitions does Jesus issue to his followers?

9. Jesus says even the Son doesn't know the day or hour of these events (v. 32). A good deal of ancient and modern writing on prophecy tries to figure out precise timing of events, reducing the Bible to the level of a horoscope. What does this passage teach us about leaving such issues to God and trusting him when the future is not entirely clear?

10. The concluding command in this chapter is not, "Sit down and work out a prophetic timetable," but instead, "Keep awake and watch!" What does Jesus mean by this command, and how can we carry it out?

PRAY

Pray for Christians around the world suffering persecution for their faith. Ask God to help you keep watch for Jesus' coming and to be faithful to him as you do so.

17

PREPARED FOR DEATH

Mark 14:1-25

On my fortieth birthday, my students gave me a surprise party. While I was taking a service in the college chapel, they carefully cleared the papers in my room, decorated it from floor to ceiling, and laid out a magnificent spread. I knew nothing about it until I walked through the door. It was a marvelous and memorable evening.

It's a deep human instinct—I believe a God-given one—that we mark significant moments with significant meals. Sharing a meal, especially a festive one, binds together a family, a group of friends, a collection of colleagues. Such meals say more than we could ever put into words about who we are, how we feel about one another, and the hopes and joys that we share together. The meal not only feeds our bodies; that seems in some ways the least significant part of it. It *says* something and it *does* something, actually changing us so that, after it, part of who we actually are is "the people who shared that meal together, with all that it meant."

OPEN

When did you share a meal with others that marked a significant moment?

STUDY

1. *Read Mark 14:1-11.* Perhaps the most significant meal in the Old Testament was Passover. Passover time was freedom time. Every year, and still to the present day, the Jewish people tell the story of the exodus from Egypt, leaving the slavery of Pharaoh and coming through the wilderness to the Promised Land. Passover, in the midst of Roman occupation, is the setting Jesus chose for the final showdown with the temple and its hierarchy.

   Why isn't Passover time a good time for the Jewish authorities to arrest Jesus?

2. While the chief priests and lawyers are plotting against Jesus, an unnamed woman is anointing him with valuable oil. How do the people present react to the woman's worship of Jesus?

3. What is Jesus' response to this woman?

4. What is Jesus saying about the poor in verse 7?

5. Jesus is not implying that the woman has any actual knowledge of

his coming fate. She has simply acted spontaneously, out of the fullness of her heart. She has, in fact, gone intuitively right to the heart of things, cutting through the male objections on the one hand, and contrasting with the male plots on the other. Not for nothing is this story sometimes held up as an example of a woman getting it right while all around her men are getting it wrong.

How do we sometimes react when people seem to worship Jesus without inhibition—pouring out their valuables, their stories, their dancing, their music—in ways we feel aren't appropriate?

6. Which group or individual do you identify with most in this scene and why?

7. *Read Mark 14:12-25.* At Passover Jews not only told the story of how God liberated them but also ate a commemorative meal together. Celebrating Passover was and is a deeply religious act, and also, for the many centuries in which Jews have suffered oppression, a deeply political act. It says, loud and clear, "despite appearances, we are God's free people." It sustains loyalty; it encourages faith, hope and love.

What do the disciples do to prepare for the Passover meal (vv. 12-16)?

8. Why does Jesus' announcement upset the disciples (vv. 17-21)?

9. How does Jesus add new meaning to two of the Passover elements (vv. 22-25)?

This Passover-meal-with-a-difference is going to *explain,* more deeply than words could ever do, what his action, and passion, the next day really meant; and, more than explaining it, it will enable Jesus' followers, from that day to this, to make it their own, to draw life and strength from it. If we want to understand, and be nourished by, what happened on Calvary, this meal is the place to start.

This meal, with all its new-passover associations, was Jesus' primary means of enabling his followers not only to understand his death but to let it do its freedom-work in their lives and in the world. It drew to a head the kingdom-actions (not least the feastings) and kingdom-teaching of his whole public career.

10. How does this meal help us make sense of Jesus' death and his kingdom that will come?

11. Different Christian traditions call this meal the Eucharist, the Lord's Supper or Communion. How can your study of this chapter enrich your participation in it?

PRAY

Thank God for the salvation that Jesus' death bought for you. Ask him to help you have a more worshipful heart like the woman who anointed Jesus with oil.

FORSAKEN AND REJECTED

Mark 14:26-72

What do you do when the strong person in your life suddenly becomes weak? Children face this when the parent on whom they have relied for everything is suddenly struck down with illness or grief. Colleagues working on a project are thrown into confusion if the team leader suddenly loses confidence. A church is dismayed if the pastor or preacher suddenly loses faith or hope or integrity.

OPEN

When did a strong person in your life become weak, and how did you respond?

STUDY

1. *Read Mark 14:26-52.* We can only imagine the effect on the disciples of the sudden change that came over Jesus in Gethsemane. Until that moment he had been in control: planning, directing, teaching, guiding. He had always been ready with a word or action. Now he is,

as we say, falling apart. But he wasn't the only one. What does Jesus predict his disciples will do in the near future (vv. 27-30)?

2. How does the response of the disciples to Jesus' prediction contrast with their response to his call to stay with him in prayer?

3. Why is prayer often so difficult for us, even with the best of intentions?

4. How would you describe Jesus' emotional state in Gethsemane (vv. 32-40)?

5. Three times Jesus prays for rescue. Three times he appears to receive the answer, No (vv. 34-41). What can we learn if even Jesus received such a response to one of his most heartfelt prayers?

6. Why is Jesus surprised that people come armed with weapons to arrest him?

7. Which person or group in this garden scene do you identify with most? Why?

8. *Read Mark 14:53-72.* How does Mark contrast Jesus and Peter (vv. 53-54, 61-62, 66-71)?

The detailed description of Peter's failure highlights the solitariness of Jesus. Betrayed by one associate, forsaken by ten more, and now publicly and bitterly renounced by his closest friend; he stands alone, defenseless, before the Jewish court, before the world. This too is important for the story Mark is telling: what Jesus has to do now, he has to do all by himself. No one else can give their life as a ransom for many. No one else can bring Israel's story of failure and redemption to its climax. If he is the Messiah, there comes a moment when he has to act solo. That moment has now arrived.

9. What different charges are leveled against Jesus (vv. 55-64)?

10. What is indicated by the way Jesus was arrested and the way the trial was conducted?

11. The judges were aware that what Jesus had done and said constituted a veiled claim to royal authority. He was making moves that could only be explained if he thought he was the true King, the Messiah. Now there was nothing wrong, let alone blasphemous, with thinking oneself to be Messiah. It wasn't a capital offense under Jewish law. Nevertheless the court knew, and Jesus knew they knew, that if someone claimed to be a king, and the Roman governor heard about it, there could only be one result. Crucifixion, though practiced widely in the Roman world for various offenses, was the standard treatment for would-be rebel leaders. Hence the chief priest's key question, when Jesus remains silent about the temple: Are you the Messiah?

It isn't that Jesus has, as it were, claimed simply to be divine. It is, rather, that the two biblical texts he drew on (Psalm 110 and Daniel 7:13), taken together, answer all the questions simultaneously, and add to them the assertion that Jesus will be vindicated, exalted to a place at God's right hand. The answer says, in a tight-packed phrase: yes, I am a true prophet; yes, what I said about the temple will come true; yes, I am the Messiah; *you will see me vindicated;* and my vindication will mean that I share the very throne of Israel's God. At last the masks are off, the secrets are out, the cryptic sayings and parables are left behind. The Son of Man stands before the official ruler of Israel declaring that God will prove him in the right and the court in the wrong.

How do Peter's and Jesus' actions and words illustrate Mark 8:35: "If you want to save your life, you'll lose it; but if you lose your life because of me and the Message you'll save it"?

12. In what ways might you be called to lose your life for Jesus and the good news of the gospel?

PRAY

Ask God to help you follow Jesus' example of losing your life for him instead of trying to hang onto it.

19

CONDEMNED
AND CRUCIFIED

Mark 15:1-39

Sometimes words fail us. As T. S. Eliot wryly observed, they slip and slide and will not stay in place. We are too used to them, as many Christians are too used to the story of Jesus' death. We need, regularly, to find ways of making the story strange again, unfamiliar, so we can hear it once more as though it were new. Indeed it is a strange story full of the unexpected, the ironic, the disturbing.

OPEN

In what situation have words failed you or someone else in trying to express something important?

STUDY

1. *Read Mark 15:1-15.* The cross was a political symbol long before it became a religious symbol. Pilate knew, the crowds knew, the chief

priests knew, and Jesus knew, what it meant. It was the ultimate symbol of Roman power. It said, "We are in charge here, and this is what happens to people who get in our way."

How does Jesus respond to his accusers (vv. 1-5)?

2. Pilate wasn't looking to crucify Jesus. What different motivations that Pilate has are revealed by his questions and actions (vv. 6-15)?

Pilate might have flogged an errant prophet if he was causing trouble. He would have dismissed a blasphemy case with a flick of his hand. But would-be kings spelled political trouble. This was the charge he had to take notice of, even though he knew Jesus wasn't leading the normal sort of messianic revolt (he didn't bother to round up any of his followers). Mark wants to be sure that we think of Jesus' death in terms of his messiahship, confronting the power of Rome, built as it was on the power of death.

3. How does the Barabbas story help us understand some of the signifi-cance of Jesus' crucifixion?

4. What is your reaction to God's grace shown in this incident?

5. *Read Mark 15:16-39.* Mark builds up the story of Jesus' crucifixion through small pictures, one detail after another that together tell the story in a clipped sequence, moving swiftly from scene to scene. What short snapshots does Mark capture in verses 16-32?

6. What do they teach us about Jesus' death?

7. What is ironic about the taunts people make to Jesus as he hangs on the cross?

The main theme that emerges over and over is that Jesus is cruci-fied as the King of the Jews. It is because he is bearing the fate and destiny of Israel, as its anointed representative, that his death means what it means to Mark. Israel is where the world's violence and wick-edness seem to have concentrated itself; but the Messiah, the King, has already taken it upon himself, and so has made a way of rescue, of ransom, for any who will follow him.

8. If we were reading Mark for the first time, we might expect that, after the mocking of the crowds, all that would be left would be for

Jesus to die. We might have imagined that this would take some time, since crucified people often hovered between life and death for days, and (as John's Gospel informs us in 19:31-34) only the imminent arrival of the Jewish sabbath would make the soldiers finish off the job more quickly. But nothing could have prepared us for the bizarre events that Mark relates in this short account of Jesus' last minutes.

What happens right before Jesus dies (vv. 33-39)?

9. How is Jesus' cry in verse 34 the climax of his sufferings?

10. How does verse 38 tie in the previous four chapters of Mark?

11. While Son of Man has been the common title Jesus uses for himself, another title has made a few appearances also. First, "God's Son" is found in the opening line of Mark's Gospel (1:1). Then the voice at Jesus' baptism hails him as God's beloved Son (1:11). Evil spirits identified him the same way (3:11; 5:7). So does the voice at the transfiguration (9:7). Then the high priest asked if he was God's Son (14:61).

Why is it significant that a Roman soldier now gives him this title?

12. What difference has Jesus' death on the cross made in your life?

PRAY

Thank God for what Jesus did in dying on the cross.

20

VICTORY OVER DEATH

Mark 15:40—16:20

Yesterday a friend came to see me in great excitement. He had been in Jerusalem a few weeks earlier and had happened to be present when an archaeologist stumbled upon a previously unknown first-century tomb, just outside the walls of the old city. It was preserved intact: bones, ossuaries (bone boxes), everything, including one full skeleton still wrapped up, laid by itself in a niche in the cave. Presumably the family had not been able to return, as they normally expect to, and collect the bones to put them in another ossuary.

There are, no doubt, still plenty of other archaeological excitements waiting to be discovered.

OPEN

When have you made a surprising discovery, whether it was finding an object, understanding a new truth, getting to know someone in a new way or something else? How did that discovery affect you?

STUDY

1. *Read Mark 15:40—16:8.* What is significant about the people present for Jesus' burial (15:40-47)?

2. What do verses 42-47 tell us about Joseph?

3. What risks does Joseph run by taking responsibility for Jesus' burial?

4. Soon after Jesus' burial (and even to this day) some have claimed that Jesus didn't actually die. What details in this account confirm that he did?

5. Middle Eastern burials of this era took place in two stages. First, the body was wrapped up, covered in spices to offset the smell and then laid on a shelf in a cave. Second, a year or two later when the flesh had decomposed, the bones were then gathered into a box called an ossuary and stored in the tomb, leaving room for the burial of another family member on the now empty shelf.

   Mark finishes his account of the burial with a feeling of eager impatience. He has set everything in order for the next stage, but now it is the sabbath, and everything must rest, including the body of Jesus himself.

What are the women expecting when they go to the tomb (16:1-3)?

6. Note what the women are *not* saying to themselves (as they might be if this story were a later pious fiction). They were not going to witness Jesus' resurrection. They had no idea that any such thing was even thinkable. They were going to complete the primary burial. This was a sad task, but a necessary one, both for reverence's sake, and to lessen the smell of decomposition as other bodies, in due course, might be buried in the same tomb over the coming year or so, prior to Jesus' bones being collected and put into an ossuary (the secondary burial).

What do they see instead (16:4-5)?

7. How do they respond to what they see and hear (16:6-8)?

8. In the ancient world women were regarded as worthless witnesses. Why does Mark's mention of them here actually affirm the validity of this story rather than call the events into question?

9.   What is the significance of Jesus' resurrection for you?

10. *Read Mark 16:9-20*. Mark's original ending is missing. I'm convinced
     of it. Two of our best manuscripts, both from the fourth century, end
     with verse 8. The alternative endings (the longer one is designated
     by verses 9-20) in several other manuscripts seem clearly to be later
     writings, added by copyists who, agreeing with me that Mark couldn't
     have meant to stop there, were determined to fill in the gap.

     What does this ending tell us about how early Christians saw the
     events of Easter and their significance?

11. What tasks has our risen Lord given you in order to take the gospel
     into all the world?

12. How would you evaluate your own discipleship, your commission
     from the risen Jesus?

PRAY

Thank God for what you've learned from this study of Mark. Ask him to
help you continue to follow Jesus and take the gospel to the world.

GUIDELINES FOR LEADERS

My grace is sufficient for you.
(2 Corinthians 12:9)

If leading a small group is something new for you, don't worry. These sessions are designed to flow naturally and be led easily. You may even find that the studies seem to lead themselves!

This study guide is flexible. You can use it with a variety of groups—students, professionals, coworkers, friends, neighborhood or church groups. Each study takes forty-five to sixty minutes in a group setting.

You don't need to be an expert on the Bible or a trained teacher to lead a small group. These guides are designed to facilitate a group's discussion, not a leader's presentation. Guiding group members to discover together what the Bible has to say and to listen together for God's guidance will help them remember much more than a lecture would.

There are some important facts to know about group dynamics and encouraging discussion. The suggestions listed below should equip you to effectively and enjoyably fulfill your role as leader.

PREPARING FOR THE STUDY

1. Ask God to help you understand and apply the passage in your own life. Unless this happens, you will not be prepared to lead others. Pray too for the various members of the group. Ask God to open

your hearts to the message of his Word and motivate you to action.

2. Read the introduction to the entire guide to get an overview of the topics that will be explored.

3. As you begin each study, read and reread the assigned Bible passage to familiarize yourself with it. This study guide is based on the For Everyone series on the New Testament (published by SPCK and Westminster John Knox). It will help you and the group if you have on hand a copy of the companion volume from the For Everyone series both for the translation of the passage found there and for further insight into the passage.

4. Carefully work through each question in the study. Spend time in meditation and reflection as you consider how to respond.

5. Write your thoughts and responses in the space provided in the study guide. This will help you to express your understanding of the passage clearly.

6. It may help to have a Bible dictionary handy. Use it to look up any unfamiliar words, names or places. The glossary at the end of each New Testament for Everyone commentary may likewise be helpful for keeping discussion moving.

7. Reflect seriously on how you need to apply the Scripture to your life. Remember that the group members will follow your lead in responding to the studies. They will not go any deeper than you do.

LEADING THE STUDY

1. At the beginning of your first time together, explain that these studies are meant to be discussions, not lectures. Encourage the members of the group to participate. However, do not put pressure on those who may be hesitant to speak—especially during the first few sessions.

2. Be sure that everyone in your group has a study guide. Encourage the group to prepare beforehand for each discussion by reading the introduction to the guide and by working through the questions in each study.

3. Begin each study on time. Open with prayer, asking God to help the group to understand and apply the passage.

4. Have a group member read aloud the introduction at the beginning of the discussion.

5. Discuss the "Open" question before the Bible passage is read. The "Open" question introduces the theme of the study and helps group members to begin to open up, and can reveal where our thoughts and feelings need to be transformed by Scripture. Reading the passage first will tend to color the honest reactions people would otherwise give—because they are, of course, supposed to think the way the Bible does. Encourage as many members as possible to respond to the "Open" question, and be ready to get the discussion going with your own response.

6. Have a group member read aloud the passage to be studied as indicated in the guide.

7. The study questions are designed to be read aloud just as they are written. You may, however, prefer to express them in your own words.

   There may be times when it is appropriate to deviate from the study guide. For example, a question may have already been answered. If so, move on to the next question. Or someone may raise an important question not covered in the guide. Take time to discuss it, but try to keep the group from going off on tangents.

8. Avoid answering your own questions. An eager group quickly becomes passive and silent if members think the leader will do most of the talking. If necessary repeat or rephrase the question until it is clearly understood, or refer to the commentary woven into the guide to clarify the context or meaning.

9. Don't be afraid of silence in response to the discussion questions. People may need time to think about the question before formulating their answers.

10. Don't be content with just one answer. Ask, "What do the rest of you think?" or "Anything else?" until several people have given answers to the question.

11. Try to be affirming whenever possible. Affirm participation. Never reject an answer; if it is clearly off-base, ask, "Which verse led you to that conclusion?" or again, "What do the rest of you think?"

12. Don't expect every answer to be addressed to you, even though this will probably happen at first. As group members become more at ease, they will begin to truly interact with each other. This is one sign of healthy discussion.

13. Don't be afraid of controversy. It can be very stimulating. If you don't resolve an issue completely, don't be frustrated. Explain that the group will move on and God may enlighten all of you in later sessions.

14. Periodically summarize what the group has said about the passage. This helps to draw together the various ideas mentioned and gives continuity to the study. But don't preach.

15. Conclude your time together with the prayer suggestion at the end of the study, adapting it to your group's particular needs as appropriate. Ask for God's help in following through on the applications you've identified.

16. End on time.

Many more suggestions and helps for studying a passage or guiding discussion can be found in *How to Lead a LifeGuide Bible Study* and *The Big Book on Small Groups* (both from InterVarsity Press/USA).

Other InterVarsity Press Resources from N. T. Wright

The Challenge of Jesus
N. T. Wright offers clarity and a full accounting of the facts of the life and
teachings of Jesus, revealing how the Son of God was also solidly planted in
first-century Palestine. *978-0-8308-2200-3, 202 pages, hardcover*

Resurrection
This 50-minute DVD confronts the most startling claim of Christianity—that
Jesus rose from the dead. Shot on location in Israel, Greece and England, N. T.
Wright presents the political, historical and theological issues of Jesus' day and
today regarding this claim. Wright brings clarity and insight to one of the most
profound mysteries in human history. Study guide included.
978-0-8308-3435-8, DVD

Evil and the Justice of God
N. T. Wright explores all aspects of evil and how it presents itself in society
today. Fully grounded in the story of the Old and New Testaments, this presentation is provocative and hopeful; a fascinating analysis of and response to the
fundamental question of evil and justice that faces believers.
978-0-8308-3398-6, 176 pages, hardcover

Evil
Filmed in Israel, South Africa and England, this 50-minute DVD confronts some
of the major "evil" issues of our time—from tsunamis to AIDS—and puts them
under the biblical spotlight. N. T. Wright says there is a solution to the problem
of evil, if only we have the honesty and courage to name it and understand it for
what it is. Study guide included. *978-0-8308-3434-1, DVD*

Justification: God's Plan and Paul's Vision
In this comprehensive account and defense of the crucial doctrine of justification, Wright also responds to critics who have challenged what has come to be
called the new perspective. Ultimately, he provides a chance for those in the
middle of and on both sides of the debate to interact directly with his views and
form their own conclusions. *978-0-8308-3863-9, 279 pages, hardcover*

Colossians and Philemon
In Colossians, Paul presents Christ as "the firstborn over all creation," and ap-
peals to his readers to seek a maturity found only Christ. In Philemon, Paul ap-
peals to a fellow believer to receive a runaway slave in love and forgiveness. In
this volume N. T. Wright offers comment on both of these important books.
978-0-8308-4242-1, 199 pages, paperback